EYE TO EYE WITH DOGS

MALTESE

Lynn M. Stone

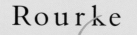
Rourke
Publishing LLC
Vero Beach, Florida 32964

www.rourkepublishing.com

PHOTO CREDITS: All photos © Lynn M. Stone

Editor: Meg Greve

Cover and page design by Nicola Stratford

Library of Congress Cataloging-in-Publication Data

Stone, Lynn M.
  Maltese / Lynn M. Stone.
      p. cm. -- (Eye to eye with dogs)
  Includes index.
  ISBN 978-1-60472-365-6
  1. Maltese dog--Juvenile literature. I. Title.
  SF429.M25S76 2009
  636.76--dc22

                              2008012976

Printed in the USA

CG/CG

Rourke Publishing

www.rourkepublishing.com – rourke@rourkepublishing.com
Post Office Box 3328, Vero Beach, FL 32964

Table of Contents

The little Maltese is one of the many toy breeds.

The Maltese

The Maltese is a little dog with a big, soft white coat. Even a 12-inch (30-centimeter) ruler standing on end is taller than a Maltese.

The Maltese is one of the oldest dog **breeds**. Today, as in the past, people love the Maltese largely as a household pet. No wonder the Maltese is a **companion** dog. It is gentle and **affectionate**.

MALTESE FACTS

Weight: 4 to 6 pounds (2 to 3 kilograms)
Height: 8 to 10 inches (20 to 25 centimeters)
Country of Origin: Malta and Mediterranean region
Life Span: 12 to 14 years

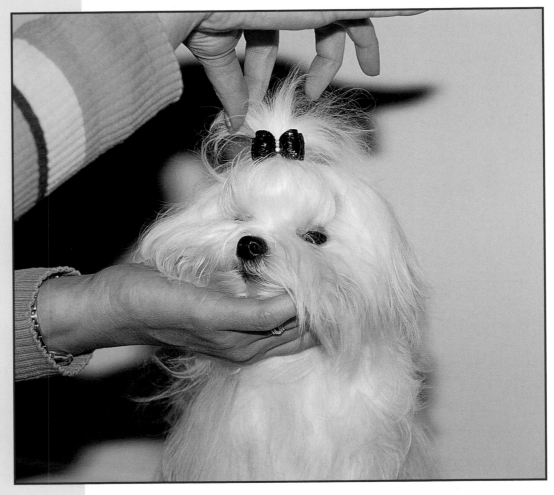

Topknots are a popular hairstyle for many small, long-haired breeds.

A Maltese owner often ties the hair of the dog's head into a **topknot**. The topknot helps keep the silky hair neat. It also allows the dog to see more clearly.

A Maltese likes a warm lap or couch, but it is not a couch potato. It is alert, quick, and active.

Bright eyes and a playful personality are typical of the Maltese.

The Yorkshire terrier is another popular breed in the toy group.

The American Kennel Club lists Maltese in the toy dog group. Toys are small dogs, such as miniature poodles, Yorkshire terriers, and Pomeranians.

Looks

A Maltese in full coat seems to be wearing a long, silky gown. The gown of hair reaches from the dog's back to the ground!

Maltese owners love their dogs' long coats.

A Maltese's nose and eyes are like black buttons in a sea of white. A Maltese may have some tan or lemon color on its ears, but **show judges** prefer perfectly white dogs.

Unlike many breeds, the Maltese has a coat of just one color: white.

A Maltese's dark nose and eyes contrast with its snowy fur.

Head held high, a Maltese seems to walk proudly.

A Maltese moves smoothly, its head held high. The dog carries its fluffy tail gracefully over its **hindquarters**. The legs almost disappear under its long blanket of hair.

The Maltese are known to be gentle and content to be around children.

Maltese of the Past

Ancient dog lovers probably developed the Maltese more than 3,000 years ago.

Dog breeds do not just suddenly appear. They result from people making choices. People take certain dogs they like, for one reason or another, and **mate** them to each other.

Some owners show the best of the breed in competitions.

It is likely that Phoenician traders brought dogs much like the modern Maltese to Malta more than 2,000 years ago. Malta is an island in the Mediterranean Sea off the southern coast of Italy.

The little white dogs became popular with wealthy people in Malta. Well dressed women carried them in their sleeves and on their laps. During this time, Pubilius, the Roman governor of Malta, had a Maltese named Issa.

The Maltese's ancestors may have included one or more types of spaniels.

The modern Maltese may partly be the result of people having **crossed** miniature poodles and spaniels. Spaniels are a family of small and medium sized dogs first developed in Spain and later bred in several varieties by the British.

The Dog for You?

The Maltese is a popular breed for many reasons. It is friendly, playful, trusting, gentle, and cute. It is comfortable in a small house. The Maltese is patient with children, too.

The Maltese makes a wonderful pet for people of all ages.

Maltese are dogs of hearth and home.

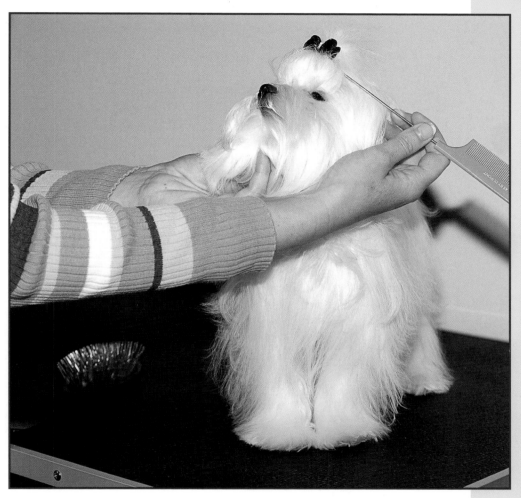

Grooming helps keep the coat of this Maltese silky.

Despite its long hair, the Maltese is not a heavy shedder. The long outer coat of a Maltese does not have an undercoat. That helps to reduce shedding. Still, a Maltese requires almost daily hair care.

Grooming helps prevent its long hair from tangling and matting. If you own a Maltese, you will need to be willing to comb the dog's long, silky hair.

A shorter haircut keeps a Maltese cool in the summer.

20

Owner and pooch both benefit from a walk.

The Maltese is an active breed. A happy Maltese needs attention along with walks and playtime exercise.

Some Maltese bark often and easily, but that is not all bad. Barking dogs usually make great watchdogs.

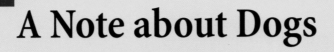

A Note about Dogs

Puppies are cute and cuddly, but only after serious thought should anybody buy one. Puppies, after all, grow up.

A dog will require more than love and patience. It will need healthy food, exercise, grooming, medical care, and a warm, safe place to live.

A dog can be your best friend, but you need to be its best friend, too.

Choosing the right breed for you requires homework. For more information about buying and owning a dog, contact the American Kennel Club or the Canadian Kennel Club.

Glossary

affectionate (uh-FEK-shuh-nuht): friendly, loving

breeds (BREEDS): particular kinds of domestic animals within a larger, closely related group, such as the Maltese within the dog group

companion (kuhm-PAN-yuhn): a friend

crossed (KRAWST): to have been matched to another breed for the purpose of producing pups

hindquarters (HINDE-kwor-turz): the rear portion of a dog, including its rear legs

mate (MAYT): to place a female and male dog together to produce pups

show judges (SHOH juhj-is): those people who choose winners at various kinds of dog shows

topknot (TOP-not): the hair at the top of a dog's head tied up with a bow or clip

Index

Further Reading

Fernandez, Amy. *Maltese*. TFH Publications, 2007.
Furstinger, Nancy. *Maltese*. ABDO, 2006.
American Kennel Club. *The Complete Dog Book*. American Kennel
    Club, 2006.

Website to Visit

http://www.akc.org/breeds/maltese
www.americanmaltese.org
www.nextdaypets.com/directory/breeds/1100167

About the Author

Lynn M. Stone is a widely-published wildlife and domestic animal
photographer and the author of more than 500 children's books.
His book *Box Turtles* was chosen as an Outstanding Science Trade
Book and Selectors' Choice for 2008 by the Science Committee of
the National Science Teachers' Association and the Children's
Book Council.